Ms. Fitzgerald

S.67

copy 1 C.H.

553.2/
Ri d

Ridpath
Man and materials:
GAS

Discard.

DEMCO

Man and Materials Series

Man and Materials: COAL
Man and Materials: GAS
Man and Materials: MINERALS
Man and Materials: OIL
Man and Materials: PLASTICS
Man and Materials: STONE

An Addisonian Press Book

First published in the United States 1975, by Addison-Wesley
All rights reserved. No part of this book may
be reproduced in any form without the permission
of Addison-Wesley Publishing Company, Inc.
Reading, Massachusetts 01867
© 1975 Macmillan Education Limited of London
Designed by Robert Updegraff
Printed in Spain
First Printing

Photographic Acknowledgements
Amoco Europe Incorporated; British Gas Corporation; Gas
Council; Goodyear Tyre and Rubber Co.; I.C.I.;
Kellogg International Corporation; Mansell Collection;
Science Museum, Shell; Robert Updegraff;
J. Walter Thompson Co.

Library of Congress Cataloging in Publication Data
Ridpath, Ian.
    Man and materials: gas.
    SUMMARY: An introduction to fuel gas including the
origin and production of natural gas and a variety of
man-made gases and their present and future uses.
    1. Gas, Natural—Juvenile literature. 2. Gas as
fuel—Juvenile literature. [1. Gas] I. Title.
TN880.R49 1975   553'.285   74-10540
ISBN 0-201-09031-7

Man and Materials

GAS

compiled under the general editorship of Ian Ridpath

▲▼ Addison·Wesley

Types of Gas

Gases are the least dense form of matter. Air is a gas, or rather a mixture of several different gases. But this book is about *fuel gas*—the gas we can burn to provide heat. There are several different types of fuel gas.

Natural gas is extracted from under the ground where it has been for millions of years. Natural gas is mostly *methane*, which is made up of carbon and hydrogen. In methane, four atoms of hydrogen combine with one of carbon.

A lot of the gas used in the world today is natural gas. But the first type of gas to be widely used was manufactured from coal. It is called town or city gas in various parts of the world because it was the type first supplied for lighting and heating in towns. It contains mostly hydrogen, plus some methane and carbon combined with oxygen.

NATURAL G

TOWN GAS

4¼ cubic meters of air

9½ cubic meters of

1 cubic meter of gas

1 cubic meter of g

The air needed to burn a cubic meter of town gas and natural gas. The same volume of natural gas gives twice the heat.

2

Gas made from coal does not burn in quite the same way as natural gas. A gas-burning appliance, such as a stove, has to be adapted if a different form of gas is connected to it. In order to burn properly, natural gas needs more than twice as much air as manufactured gas does. Without the extra air, natural gas gives a yellow, sooty flame — a result of incomplete burning.

Natural gas has twice the *calorific value* of town or city gas. This means that only half the amount of gas is needed to provide the same amount of heat.

Above: A modern natural gas burner.
Below: Using natural gas in China about 300 AD.

Burners

Bamboo pipes

Natural gas source

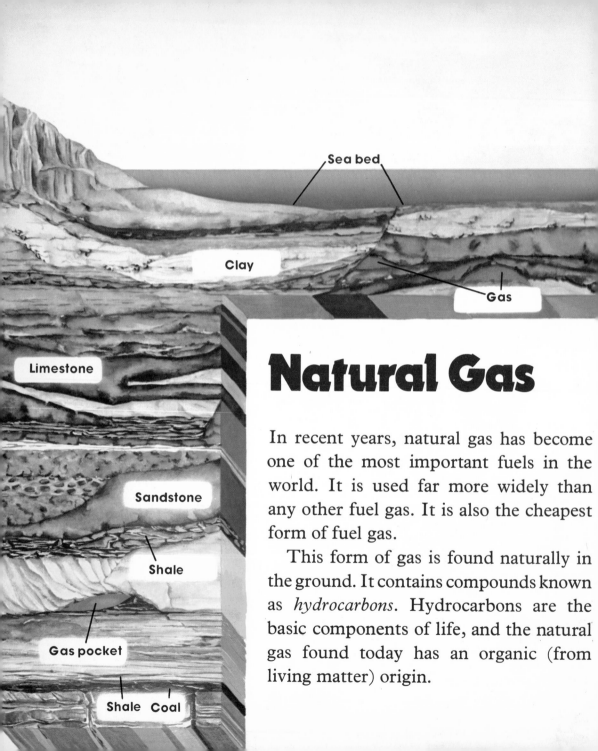

Sea bed

Clay

Gas

Limestone

Sandstone

Shale

Gas pocket

Shale Coal

Natural Gas

In recent years, natural gas has become one of the most important fuels in the world. It is used far more widely than any other fuel gas. It is also the cheapest form of fuel gas.

This form of gas is found naturally in the ground. It contains compounds known as *hydrocarbons*. Hydrocarbons are the basic components of life, and the natural gas found today has an organic (from living matter) origin.

Left: Natural gas lies in rocks that are porous (filled with small holes). Pockets of natural gas can collect where non-porous rock prevents the gas from seeping out. Underground pockets can be difficult to find.

Below: A fault in the rock formation may trap a pocket of gas.

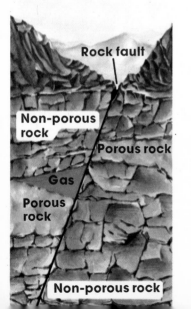

Rock fault

Non-porous rock

Porous rock

Gas

Porous rock

Non-porous rock

Oil contains more complicated hydrocarbons than natural gas. The compounds of which it is made are denser, and therefore oil is found in liquid form. Natural gas is often found in conjunction with oil. But it can be found on its own.

Tiny creatures decayed to form natural gas. They lived in the sea hundreds of millions of years ago. When they died, they sank to the bottom along with other dead organic matter such as plants. In time, these remains were covered with sand and mud. Pressure from the mud and sand layers, and heat from the Earth helped to break down the organic matter into simple molecules containing hydrogen and carbon.

Many of these molecules formed gas. When the rock above the gas was porous (containing tiny spaces) the gas could slowly rise. In some places, the gas became trapped under layers of non-porous rock. The trapped gas filled the spaces in the porous rock.

Finding Natural Gas

Natural gas can become trapped underground where there are upward folds in the rock layers. This can also occur in regions where the layers have suddenly overlapped.

Because the land and sea have changed since the gas fields were formed, the geologists need to look under both land and sea during their surveys.

Above: (1) a geophone, used to record shock waves from a seismic explosion. (2) dynamite for seismic explosions.

Below: Shock waves from the seismic explosion are recorded by microphones near the surface.

Geophone

Dynamite

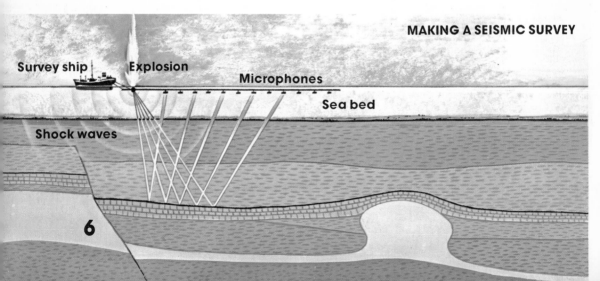

MAKING A SEISMIC SURVEY

Survey ship

Explosion

Microphones

Sea bed

Shock waves

The first general survey is made from an aircraft. Instruments measure slight changes in the gravitational pull and magnetic field of the Earth. These changes are caused by different rocks under that part of the surface.

Geologists then study these areas in detail by means of a seismic survey, in which a series of explosive charges are set off. The rock echoes reveal whether the layers of rock in the area are suitable for trapping gas.

Only drilling, however, can prove that gas is actually there.

Above: Compressed-air guns for setting up shock waves in water.

Below: The recorded shock waves from the seismic explosion are processed to make a chart which gives a picture of the layers of rock.

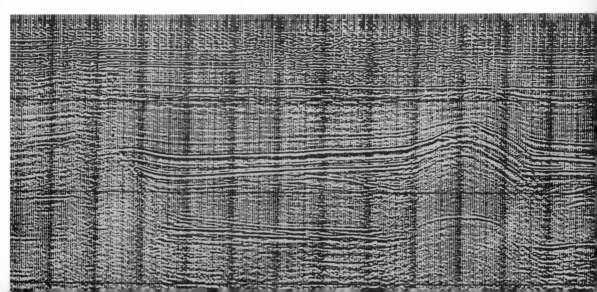

Drilling for Gas

Above: A gas rig.

Above right: The derrick.

Below: Adding new piping.

Drilling for gas is much like drilling for oil. A large tower, called a derrick, is set up over the chosen place. A hole is cut by a drill bit with strong teeth. As this sinks deeper, fresh sections of drill pipe, each nine meters long, are added to drive the bit. The last length of drill pipe to be added is turned by a rotating table on the floor of the derrick. Occasionally, when the bit wears out, all the pipe has to be disconnected and taken out so that a new drill bit can be put on.

As the drill bites deeper and deeper, metal casings are used to line the hole. A chemical liquid called 'mud' is pumped down in the drill pipe to cool the bit. The mud returns to the surface between the

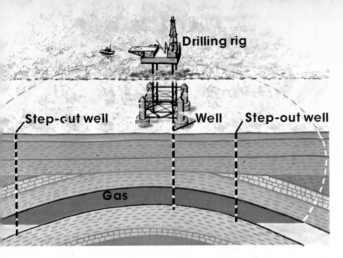

Drilling rig

Step-cut well   Well   Step-out well

Gas

Left: Discovering the extent of the gas field.

Below: Sea drilling rigs

Fixed platform

drill pipe and the casing, bringing up rock fragments and sealing the sides of the hole.

Many searches for gas are made under the sea, on the continental shelf which surrounds the land. Special drilling rigs have to be used for these situations. When drilling under water, a steel conductor pipe is first driven into the sea bed to prevent water from entering the bore hole.

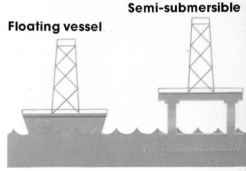

Floating vessel   **Semi-submersible**

It may be necessary to drill down for several kilometers to discover if gas is present. If it is, 'step-out' wells are drilled around the original one. The step-out wells show how far the gas field extends.

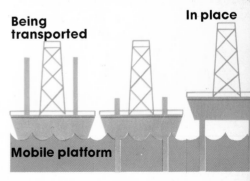

Being transported   **In place**

Mobile platform

9

Processing Gas

A gas field has to be capable of producing natural gas for many years for it to be economically worthwhile. Occasionally, the rock has to be weakened by acids, pressure, or explosions to help the gas escape.

At the site of a suitable gas field, several production wells are drilled from one platform by guiding the drill slightly sideways as it bores new holes. These extra holes are drilled to increase the gas flow to the surface.

Above: A production platform set up to pipe gas ashore from a well.

Below: An undersea pipeline connects the platform and terminal.

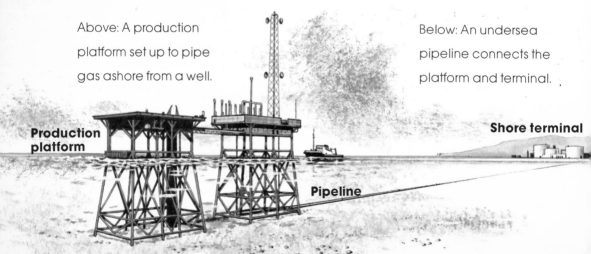

Production platform

Shore terminal

Pipeline

Natural gas is mainly methane but it contains unwanted gases that do not burn, such as carbon dioxide, nitrogen, and helium. These gases have to be removed by chemical processes. Hydrogen sulphide is also frequently found with natural gas, and produces what is called a *sour gas*. Gas with this removed is called a *sweet gas*. The methane is also accompanied by heavier hydrocarbons, such as ethane, propane, and butane. These are often removed and sold as petroleum gas. Pure methane has no smell, so a little strong-smelling chemical is added to warn users if gas is escaping.

Water and oil may also be present, and these are removed in separation tanks as near to the well head as possible. In the case of offshore platforms, an unmanned control plant is set up to pump the gas ashore. The major processing of the gas takes place at the onshore terminal. At wells on land, the gas can be processed directly at the well head.

The shore terminal where gas from an undersea well is cleaned by processing equipment.

Transporting Gas

(At top) laying a gas pipe-line on land and (above) sliding one down a ramp from a barge at sea.

After it has been processed, the dry, clean gas can be transported. Gas is sent out from some production areas for use long distances away. The natural gas is liquefied by cooling it to −165°C and putting it under pressure. In this way, 620 times as much gas can be put into a

Gantry for pumping LNG to the ship

given space. Special ships, called LNG (liquefied natural gas) carriers, are used. They have insulated tanks in which the gas is kept liquefied.

On land, the gas is distributed by a pipeline. It is pumped along under very high pressure. Liquefied methane is turned back into a gas before being sent down the pipeline. 'Mains artery' pipelines are made of welded steel sections, about a meter in diameter. Distribution stations control the flow along the pipelines. Gas is supplied locally at low pressure along smaller pipelines. Sometimes these pipes are made of plastics.

Pipeline laying should not disturb the countryside. You may never see a gas pipeline, because it has been buried under a field where crops are now growing. With off-shore rigs, they are buried in the sea bed to protect them from damage.

Above: Loading LNG into a sea-going tanker.

Below: Inside one of the insulated tanks.

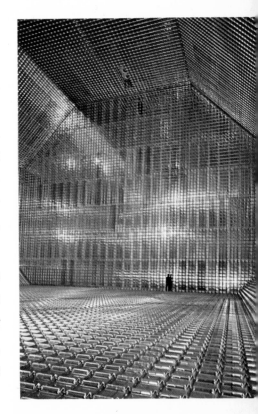

13

Coal Gas

The basic principle of making gas from coal is the same as that pioneered by William Murdoch in the 1790's. It uses heat to break down coal into gas and the spongy mass called coke. Coke is simply coal with most of the gas removed, and it consists mainly of carbon. This process, with the release of coal gas, is called *carbonization* of coal.

The crude coal gas produced by this method contains many unwanted substances. They include tar and such chemicals as ammonia and hydrogen sulphide. These give the gas its dense

Below: To make coal gas, coal is loaded into a chamber called a retort, and heated to about 1,000° Celsius. At this temperature, a thick brown gas is driven off. The retort is fueled by gas. The coal remains in the retort for about 12 hours. More coal can be loaded into the top of the retort, and the coke raked out at the base.

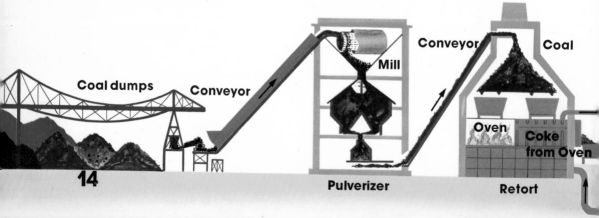

Coal dumps   Conveyor   Mill   Conveyor   Coal   Oven   Coke from Oven

Pulverizer   Retort

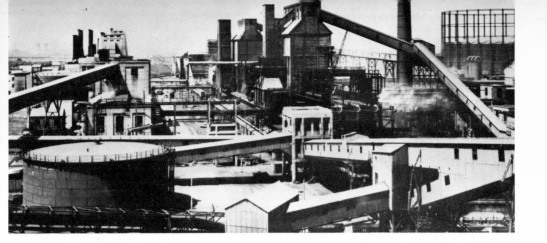

Above: A plant for producing coal gas.

Below: To remove the impurities from coal gas, a series of towers are used, called scrubbers and purifiers. Some of the chemicals that are removed from coal gas are valuable, and can be sold separately.

appearance and choking smell. They must be removed before the gas can be used.

A gas similar to coal gas is made at steelworks. It is called coke-oven gas, because it comes from the ovens in which coal is burned to make coke for use in blast furnaces. Because the steelmen particularly want the coke, they use a different type of coal from the gasworks. But coke-oven gas can be processed to make gas for burning in homes.

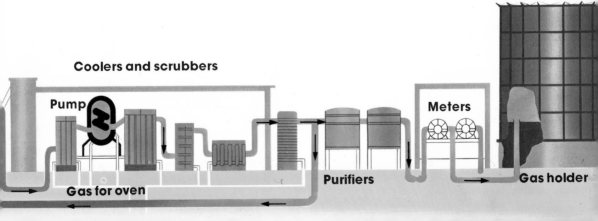

Coolers and scrubbers

Pump

Meters

Gas for oven

Purifiers

Gas holder

Pump **Tar extractor** **Purifiers** **Meters** **Scrubber** **Gas holder**

Temporary holder

Cooler

Coke **Rich gas** **Washer**

Steam

Coke **Carbureter**

Making carbureted water gas. Steam combines with carbon in coke to give carbon monoxide and hydrogen (blue water gas). Richer gas, such as natural gas or gas made from oil, is then added.

Other Man-Made Gases

There are other gases made from coal. One is water gas. It is made by blowing steam over hot coke. This gas burns with a blue flame, and so is called blue water gas. It has a lower heating value than coal gas. But it can have its heating value increased by adding richer gas. It is then called carbureted water gas.

Another gas is producer gas. This is made by blowing air over hot coke. It is easy to make, but it has a low heating value.

Neither of these two gases have been used in the home. They are not important today. More important processes turn all the coal into gas. They do not leave any

unwanted coke, and they use cheaper forms of coal, without so much gas. The most famous method is called the Lurgi process.

In this, steam and pure oxygen are blown over hot coal. This happens under a pressure 30 times greater than the Earth's atmospheric pressure. The gas produced is similar to blue water gas. It still has to be cleaned of impurities and enriched to give it a suitable heating value. The Lurgi process leaves behind only ash.

Where coal seams are too thin or poor in quality to be worth mining, scientists have tried to turn coal into gas by burning it underground. But the heating value of the gas produced has been too poor, and the experiments have stopped.

Above: A Lurgi gas plant.
Below: Air is blown through hot coke to make producer gas, a mixture of carbon monoxide and nitrogen.

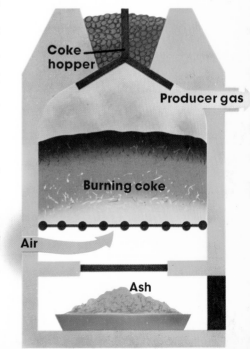

Coke hopper

Producer gas

Burning coke

Air

Ash

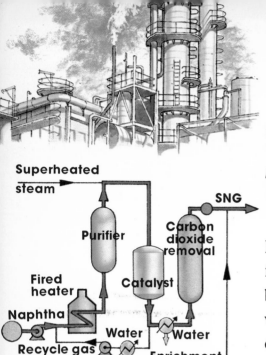

Substitute Natural Gas

Superheated steam

SNG

Purifier

Carbon dioxide removal

Catalyst

Fired heater

Naphtha

Water

Water

Recycle gas

Enrichment

Top: SNG plant.

Above: Using a catalyst

to make SNG from naphtha.

Bottom: Plant at night.

Engineers have found ways to make gas from oil. Many different kinds of gas can be made from oil. All the processes involve heating the oil so that it breaks down into gas. Usually only very light oils are used. The main one of these is called *naphtha*. Hot naphtha and steam mix together in the presence of a *catalyst*. This is a substance that helps a chemical change. In this case, the change is the

turning of steam and oil into a gas that we can burn. This process can be used to give methane gas. It is known as *substitute natural gas* (SNG).

There are other ways of making substitute natural gas. Oil and hot hydrogen gas are mixed so that they react with each other. They flow around inside a special vessel so that the hydrogen breaks the oil down into methane without a catalyst.

Oil has now become too expensive to use for much gas-making. It is also getting scarcer than coal. So engineers are developing methods of making natural gas from coal. One possible way is to take the gas from a Lurgi plant and blow it with steam over a catalyst made of nickel. This is done at a pressure of about 30 atmospheres and a temperature between 400 and 500°C.

By using the gas from a Lurgi plant in this way, the carbon and hydrogen atoms are mixed together to give almost pure methane gas.

A vessel for breaking oil into substitute natural gas without a catalyst. Light oil and hydrogen flow round inside the vessel. The hydrogen breaks down the oil to give methane.

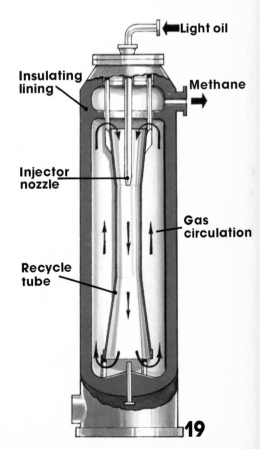

Light oil

Insulating lining

Methane

Injector nozzle

Gas circulation

Recycle tube

19

Storing Gas

Gasholders—huge upright drums for storing gas—were once a familiar sight at a gasworks. With the increasing use of natural gas, gasholders are rarely seen now. But demand for gas varies during the day and from season to season. Therefore, some gas has to be stored to meet extra demand.

There are some small storage tanks above ground in which natural gas is kept under high pressure. Often, extra gas can be 'packed' into gas mains by using a higher pressure than normal. Some underground pipes have been laid just to store extra gas. Such a system can meet changes in demand during a day.

However, there may be sudden peak demands which last a much longer time. This happens particularly in cold weather. These demands are met by bulk storage of the gas. This process can be most

Right: Unloading LNG from a tanker into storage tanks at a shore terminal in Japan.

Below: Storing gas underground in porous rock (an aquifer).

Below right: An underground storage tank made by freezing the earth.

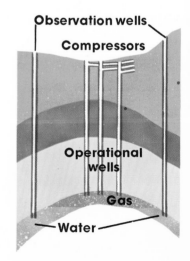

Observation wells

Compressors

Operational wells

Gas

Water

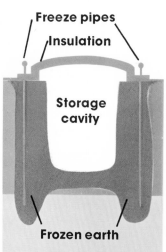

Freeze pipes

Insulation

Storage
cavity

Frozen earth

economically carried out by liquefying the gas and storing it in insulated tanks.

Engineers can even make local artificial gas fields. Old gas wells can be filled with new gas, or water trapped underground in porous rock (an *aquifer*) can be replaced by pumping in gas. Where there are no suitable underground structures, a gas-tight cavity can be made by dissolving salt deposits.

Above: A model of Frederick
Winsor demonstrating gas
lighting at a lecture.
Below: William Murdoch
lighting his house by gas.

Gas in the Past

Escapes of natural gas probably produced
the 'eternal flames' of legend. The Chinese
are thought to have been the first to make
use of this gas.

During the seventeenth century, it was
discovered that gas could be made from
coal. William Murdoch, a Scottish en-
gineer, lit his home in Cornwall with this
gas in 1792. In London, the German
Frederick Winsor used gas to light public
streets, such as The Mall (1807). During

the nineteenth century, large gasworks were built to make gas from coal, and its use for lighting spread.

About 1850, it was found that mixing air with the gas produced a strong, hot flame that could be used for cooking. At the same time, gas was used to drive the first internal combustion engines for factories, road vehicles, and electric generators. Later, gas geysers for heating water were introduced. Gas lighting was improved by 'gas mantles' which, heated in a flame, gave out a brilliant glow.

In America, the first well for natural gas was sunk by William Hart near Buffalo, New York. He supplied gas to nearby houses for lighting. In the twentieth century, natural gas replaced manufactured gas as the main supply source. Today, it is widely used for energy.

Above: The Westminster gas works, London, in 1858. The coal is being loaded into the retorts.
Below: A wall-mounted gas burner of the same period.

Water
tank

Water
heater

Warm
air
duct

Stove

Refrigerator

Central
heating

Fire

Uses of Gas

Left: Some of the many uses of gas in the home. These include heating, cooking, and refrigeration. The discovery of natural gas in many areas has led to an increase in the use of gas for domestic purposes.

Top right: Warm air from a gas-fired heating system helps the growth of roses under glass in Nice, France.

Center right: Some pottery kilns use natural gas to fire the ovens.

Below right: Cooking by bottled gas on a junk in Hong Kong harbor.

Products from Gas

Products from gas include: polystyrene granules for packaging (above), as well as bathtubs (above right), and fertilizers (below).

Gas, like oil, is an important source of chemicals. The chemicals produced from natural gas include car anti-freeze, detergents, fertilizers, herbicides and pesticides, and ammonia. Plastics and man-made fibres are also produced from the hydrocarbons in natural gas. Sulphur and helium, which are often found with natural gas, are extracted by chemicals at the well head.

A slightly denser gas than methane is also found in natural gas wells. It is called ethane. One product from ethane is acetylene gas, used in oxyacetylene torches for welding and cutting.

Equally important are the industrial processes that rely on gas for their fuel. Gas, for instance, provides part of the energy to generate electricity and produce steel. When gas is made from coal, the coke that is left behind makes a valuable smokeless fuel.

With half the world underfed, scientists have found ways of making protein from natural gas. Protein is vital because it is the structural material of living things. Some microbes can live on methane, with water added, and they produce 'single-cell' protein that could be used as a nutritious food. Whether it will be economical to use natural gas in this way is uncertain. But this is just one of the applications which underline the increasing value of natural gas as a raw material in the modern world.

Above: A plant for making ammonia from natural gas.
Below: The airship 'Goodyear Europa' which is filled with helium gas obtained from a natural-gas well.

World Distribution

Amount of gas produced
in millions of cubic
meters per month.

Argentina	515
Australia	457
Canada	7,824
Czechoslovakia	647
France	1,132
East Germany	400
West Germany	2,891
Hungary	424
Iran	1,517
Italy	1,423
Japan	622
Mexico	1,558
Netherlands	4,934
Poland	1,063
Romania	2,272
UK	3,196
USA	55,317
USSR	18,449

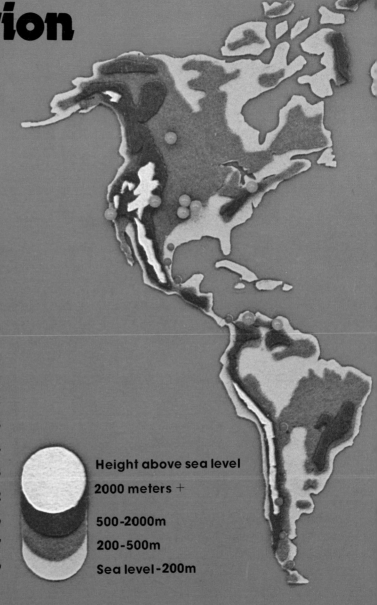

Height above sea level

2000 meters +

500-2000m

200-500m

Sea level-200m

MAJOR
CONCENTRATIONS   MINOR
CONCENTRATIONS

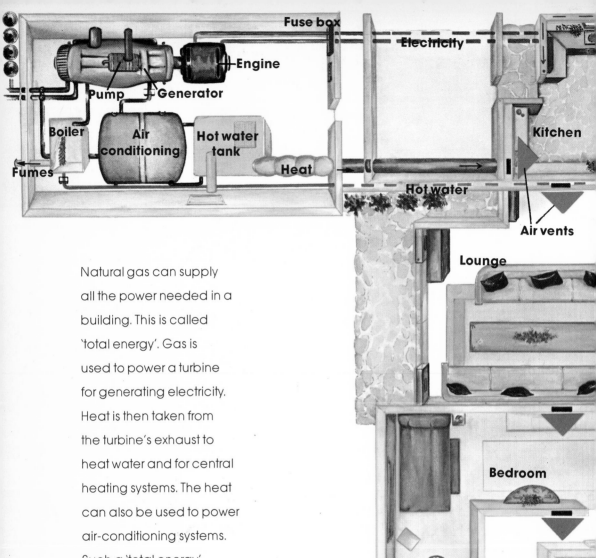

Fuse box

Electricity

Engine

Pump **Generator**

Boiler

Air conditioning

Hot water tank

Heat

Fumes

Hot water

Kitchen

Air vents

Lounge

Bedroom

Bedroom

Natural gas can supply
all the power needed in a
building. This is called
'total energy'. Gas is
used to power a turbine
for generating electricity.
Heat is then taken from
the turbine's exhaust to
heat water and for central
heating systems. The heat
can also be used to power
air-conditioning systems.
Such a 'total energy'
system minimizes the
amount of waste heat lost
from a building. Also, of
course, it is very
economical on fuel.

30

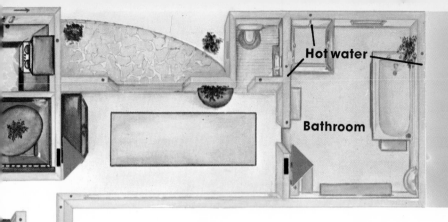

Hot water

Bathroom

Hallway

Gas in the Modern World

Natural gas is a popular fuel because it is clean. The use of natural gas is one way in which we can keep our towns free from smoke and sulphur dioxide, which damage health and darken and corrode buildings. Methane is also a particularly safe gas, because it is not poisonous.

Some of the most exciting applications of gas lie in the future. New ways of using gas are being developed all the time. One area of research is how to produce electricity from methane.

Methane can be made from sewage and other organic waste products.

18% 1975

17% 1965

13% 1955

10% 1945

5% 1935

Gas in the Future

Natural gas will not last forever. In the United States, reserves are already running low and there seems little chance of finding more gas close to the main centers of consumption. Some liquefied natural gas can be imported from abroad, but natural gas may run out at the start of the next century. We shall still want to use methane because of its cleanness and high heating value. So probably substitute natural gas will be blended with methane.

Eventually, we shall have to use only manufactured gas. But it will be substitute natural gas, made in a very different way from the dirty, smelly coal gas process that once made industrial towns so unpleasant and ugly.

Left: Natural gas is providing more and more of our fuel.

Index